# Believe in Yourself

To Rena
Get Well
love
Bruce June

# Believe in Yourself

A **Heartwarmers**™
Gift Book

WPL

# Believe in Yourself

A Heartwarmers™ Gift Book

©WPL 2002

Text by A. Fisher

Illustration by Michael Hodgkinson & Clare Lake

Printed in China

Published by WPL 2002

ISBN 1-904264-08-5

For information on other Heartwarmers™ gift books, gifts and greetings cards, please contact
WPL
14 Victoria Ind. Est. Wales Farm Road
London W3 6UU UK
Tel: +44 (0) 208 993 7268 Fax: +44 (0) 208 993 8041
email: wpl@atlas.co.uk

# Believe in yourself

This little book is for you
as I want you to know
that I believe in you,
and I hope that you will always
believe in yourself too.

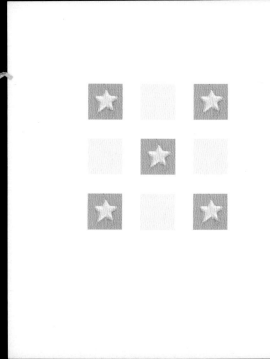

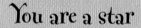

# You are a star

You can never shine too brightly.
You are an amazing person
and have the potential to succeed
at whatever you choose to do.

Just keep believing
that you deserve good things
and good things will come to you.
It is your destiny to be happy,
to find peace and contentment.

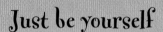

# Just be yourself

You are a special person
with unique qualities
to offer the world
just by being yourself.

You have a big heart and
inspire others with your
zest for life and determination.

# Follow your dreams

You must have dreams
in order for them to come true.
Hold onto your dreams
and never let them slip away.

Dreams give you goals to aim for
and they help to sustain you
in times of hardship.
I know you will be
rewarded with happiness.

# Trust yourself

You are perfect as you are.

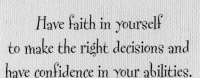

Have faith in yourself
to make the right decisions and
have confidence in your abilities.
Trust your heart and
your head to guide you.

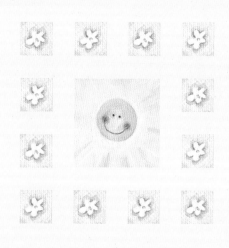

# When life gets you down

When life is an uphill struggle
it's easy to feel overwhelmed,
but every obstacle
can be an opportunity -
a lesson to be learned or
something we should let go of.

I know that you have the strength,
wisdom and perseverance
to overcome any obstacles
and achieve whatever you want.

# Don't give up

We all get tired and weary
and life can be tough
sometimes but it
doesn't last forever.
The only constant
in life is change.

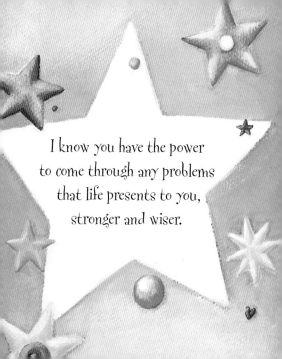

I know you have the power
to come through any problems
that life presents to you,
stronger and wiser.

# Think positively

Don't be afraid of taking the next step,
whatever it may be.
Keep a positive attitude.

All the hard work and effort
that you put in
will eventually be rewarded.

Life is a gift and full of miracles.
Just when you least expect it,
wonderful things can happen.

Expect the best not the worst,
because you deserve the best
that life can offer.

# Be kind to yourself

Give yourself the care and
compassion you show to others.
You too deserve love.

Accept yourself as you are
and try not to be too hard on yourself.

If you don't seem to
get it right first time, just try again.
I have complete confidence in you.

# I believe in you

If ever you have moments
when you doubt yourself
I want you to remember
that I believe in you.

I'm always here for you,
cheering you on.
I know what a special
person you are.

You put others' needs before your own.
You're brave in the face
of hardship and misfortune.
You are kind, considerate
and dependable.

I know that whatever you
turn your hand to,
you will do it diligently,
with focus, love and care.

Whatever you do
it will be the right thing,
whether it's big or small.

# Others believe in you

As you go your way in the world,
meeting new challenges,
confronting new situations,
remember there are people
who recognise your qualities and
abilities and who want
the very best in life for you.

We want you to be happy.

# You are not alone

When problems seem insurmountable,
reach out and the support
that you need will be there for you.
Never be afraid to ask.

Always remember that there is
an ear ready to listen to you,
a shoulder to lean on,
a helping hand and an open heart
ready to give encouragement
and support when you need it.

Never be fearful of the future
because you will always have friends.

# You are special

I want you to know
that you are a really special person -
a unique human being.

You have wonderful qualities
and a good heart which will
always see you through.

I wish you luck
and happiness
today and every day.

You're amazing and can achieve anything
in life you put your mind to.

So, wherever you go
and whatever you do,
all you have to do is...

## Believe in yourself !

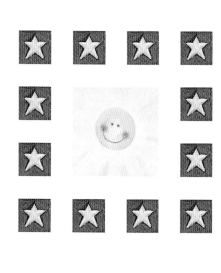

A Heartwarmers™
Gift Book

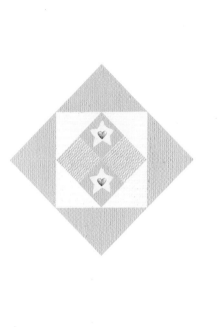

# Also available from Heartwarmers

Thank you Mum
For a Special Friend
For my Sister
For You Mum
100 Reasons why I Love You
For my Husband
To a Good Friend
For my Nan
I Love You Because...
For a Special Daughter
For a Special Mum